WASTE OF MON

JOKES BY OWEN MONEY
ILLUSTRATED BY BILL TIDY

To Murray
Best Wishes
Owen Money

BBC CYMRU WALES

WASTE OF MONEY

JOKES BY OWEN MONEY, ILLUSTRATED BY BILL TIDY

BBC *CYMRU WALES*

Published by BBC Marketing
BBC Cymru Wales
Broadcasting House
Llandaff
Cardiff CF5 2YQ

Edited and designed by Surrexit
Typeset in New Berolina and Optima
Photography by Richard Bosworth
Printed by Treforest Printing, Bedwas

ISBN 0 9518988 4 1

*T*he popular jocular humour of Owen Money is finally encaptured between the covers of his first ever book, illustrated by Bill Tidy.

His unique brand of Welsh humour has entertained audiences throughout Wales and Europe for over thirty years. His professional career began in the early 60s with his band *The Bystanders*, touring Wales and the continent. Success also followed in the 70s with his cabaret group *Tom Foolery*, topping the bill in 1979 at Blackpool's South Pier.

Permanent fame discovered Owen Money in the 1980s, followed by television performances and appearances at Cardiff's St David's Hall alongside celebrities such as Shirley Bassey.

His inimitable persona moved to BBC Radio Wales in 1987 with his Saturday morning *Money for Nothing* programme, a blend of 60s music, jokes, singing listeners and fun, counterpointing his ever popular Sunday radio slot, *Golden Money*, an insight into a cavalcade of golden hits over the past forty years.

Owen Money continues to be a firm favourite of the cabaret and pantomime stage throughout Wales and the UK, and epitomises the banterous temperament of the South Wales Valleys comic.

A man was walking through the jungle,
when he was attacked by a crocodile.
The crocodile ate the man, but the guy
was so big the croc couldn't finish him,
and left his head sticking out of its mouth.
Two Irish blokes were walking past, and
one said "Hey Paddy, that guy must be
rich - he's got a Lacoste sleeping bag!"

A man told a psychiatrist "I'm worried about my brother – he keeps thinking he's a chicken".
The psychiatrist said, "How long has this been going on?"
"About ten years," replied the man.
"Well why didn't you come sooner?" asked the psychiatrist, to which the man replied, "We needed the eggs"!!!

A man was sat at the bar one day, when he noticed on a table next to him a man playing chess with a dog. He watched for a while and was amazed when the dog actually won.
"That dog's brilliant," exclaimed the man at the bar, "you could make a fortune out of him!"
"Oh, he's not that clever," replied the chess player, "I've beaten him once or twice"!!!

Gladys and Betty were talking over
the garden wall. Gladys said to Betty,
"I buried my husband last week, he was dead".
"Never," replied Betty, "what did he die of?"
"Oh, nothing serious," answered Gladys, "only
one of those post mortem operations. If he'd had
it when he was alive, he'd be alright now"!!!

AND FURTHERMORE, MY HUSBAND'S FANCY WOMAN CAN DRINK ANY OTHER HUSBAND'S FANCY WOMAN UNDER THE TABLE!

At the firm's Christmas party, the Chairman's wife left the top table to go to powder her nose. When she returned, her husband was dancing with a gorgeous 22-year-old blonde in a mini skirt. After the dance he returned to his table. This very snobby Chairman's wife was fuming, and demanded "Who the hell was that?" "That's my fancy woman," replied the Chairman. His wife looked him right in the eye and said "That's it!" "Oh is it?" answered the Chairman. "If that's it, then that's the end of your eight weeks' holiday a year, the end of your Porsche, Mercedes and your GTi, that's the end of your American Express card and everything else that goes with it." Then the Chairman's wife noticed her husband's deputy dancing with a beautiful dark haired 20-year-old. "Who's that slut dancing with Charles?" she asked. "That's his fancy woman," answered the Chairman. "She's not as nice as ours, is she?" replied the wife!!!

I remember my dad teaching me to ride a bike,
and the day he let me go round the block on my
own his final words as I set off were,
"No messing about – ride proper."
I was a bit of a devil as a kid, and the first time
round I shouted to dad, "Look dad, no hands".
Second time round I shouted, "Look dad, no feet".
Third time round I cried, "Look dad, no teeth"!!!

Two old men were reminiscing about school.
One said "Do you know, when I was in school
I was disqualified from the walking race".
"Why's that?" asked the second man.
"Because I won it two years running" giggled
the first man!!!

My mother-in-law is such a mess. The other day she missed the rubbish man by a few seconds, and she started running after the dustcart shouting "Stop, stop, have you got room for more?" "Of course we have," replied the bin man, "jump in"!!!

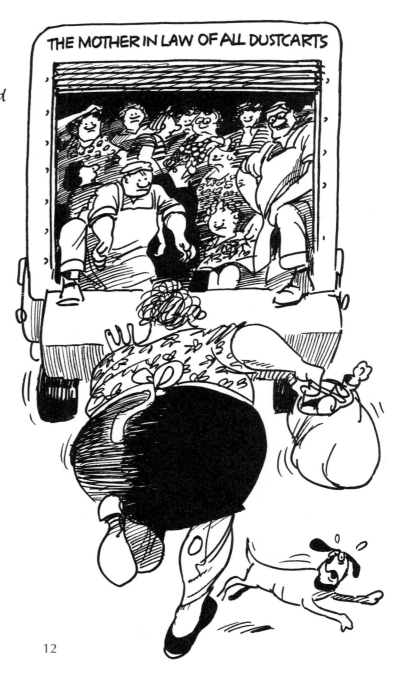

THE MOTHER IN LAW OF ALL DUSTCARTS

This gynaecologist wallpapered his hall
and stairs through the letterbox!!!

A cannibal came back from
holidays with his left arm missing.
"Did you have a nice time?" asked his mate.
"Yeah," replied the cannibal,
"but I'll never go self-catering again"!!!

A man saw the doctor after his
fingers were cut off in an accident.
The doctor said "If you'd brought them with
you, I could have sewn them back on".
"Sorry doctor," answered the man,
"but I couldn't pick them up"!!!

A man burst into the doctor's yelling, "Doctor, doctor, do something – I keep thinking I'm a tennis racquet". His doctor replied, "How long have you been highly strung?"

"Doctor, I've got this little bridge on my head, with a lovely stream flowing underneath, and on the banks of the stream there's a Chestnut tree." "Don't worry now, it's only a beauty spot"!!!

"Doctor, I've got the biggest haemorrhoid in the world." "Is that why you're sitting on a bean bag?" "Bean bag? Look again doc!"

What's got ninety balls, and makes women sweat? Bingo!

A husband and wife were going on
holidays, and got to the airport early.
As they stood in the queue, the wife said
"I wish we'd brought the piano with us".
"Why's that darling?" enquired the husband.
"Because our flight tickets are on the lid"!!!

A rather shifty-looking customer was preparing to leave a restaurant, when another man approached him and asked, "Excuse me, are you Wynford Thomas from Bedlindy?" "No I'm not," replied the shifty customer sharply. "Well I am," said the other man, "and that's his overcoat you're putting on"!!!

This fella was drinking in a pub with a giraffe.

They drank two bottles of whisky between them.

At stop tap, the giraffe keeled over, and laid the length of the bar.

The fella drank up, stepped over the giraffe and walked to the door.

"You can't leave that lyin' there," shouted the landlord after him.

The fella turned round and answered, "It's a giraffe, not a lion"!!!

What did the German watch repairer say to the broken-down watch?
"Ve have vays of making you tock!"

I went to London the other week, and got into a taxi.

"Waterloo," I said to the driver.

He answered, "The station, guv?"

I replied, "Well I'm a bit too late for the battle, mate!"

This woman was 94 and her husband was 98, and they got divorced. One of the neighbours asked them why divorce now? Their answer was "It's been on the cards for years, but we thought we'd wait for the kids to die first"!!!

This convicted murderer had been on death row for six years before the day of execution came. They strapped him into the electric chair and connected him to the mains. "Any last request?" said the penitentiary warden. "Hold my hand, will you?" replied the convict!!!

An Irishman telephoned the fire station. "Come quickly, my house is on fire!" "Okay sir, calm down," said the station officer, "how do we get to your house?" The Irishman replied, "Haven't you still got that big red fire engine?"

This couple got married, and were together on their first night in the bedroom. The fella took off his trousers, and threw them on the bed, and said to his new bride, "Put them on, love." She said "I can't do that, they're yours." "That's correct," he said. "You just remember that I wear the trousers in this house." Shocked, she took off her knickers and threw them on the bed, and said to her new husband, "Put them on." He replied, "I can't – I'll never get into them." "Quite right," she retorted, "and you never will until you change your attitude"!!!

I had gold stew for tea yesterday. It had 18 carrots in it!!!

20

Two men were talking in a pub one day, when
one asked the other what he did for a living.
"Not a lot now," answered the man. "I used
to be a human cannonball at the circus –
until they fired me"!!!

HE CAN SLEEP DOWN
HERE TILL HE FINDS
ANOTHER JOB

"My dad actually knew
the day he was going to die.
The Judge told him"!!!

A man went to see his psychiatrist.
"I must congratulate you on the progress
you're making," said the shrink.
"Progress?" replied the patient indignantly.
"Six months ago I was Napoleon, now
I'm nobody. Do you call that progress?"

A sign seen at a cemetery:
'Due to a strike, all grave digging
will be done by a skeleton crew'!!!

A baby snake in the jungle turned to his mother
one day and said worriedly, "Am I poisonous?"
"No son," said his mam.
"Thank God for that, 'cos I've just bitten my lip!"

A flasher had been caught exposing himself twenty-five times, so his mate suggested he painted himself green so that he'd merge with the bushes, and cut down the chance of being caught. He got himself a tin of green paint, painted himself from head to toe, then lay in wait for his first victim.

Along came a woman, out popped the man who flashed and then disappeared. The woman was so startled she ran across the road, but got killed by an oncoming bus. The moral of the story therefore is 'Never cross the road when the green man is flashing'!!!

A fella walked into a fish and chip shop.
"Can I have a fish?" he asked.
"It won't be long," answered the chippy.
"It had better be fat," replied the man!!!

An old woman received a gas bill of £100. She just didn't have the money, so she wrote a letter to God asking for the cash. She posted the letter and it ended up in the sorting office. One of the post office workers saw the letter addressed to God, and knew it was from someone in distress. He opened the letter and saw that this old lady was in real dire straits. So he and his mates had a whip-round and raised £95. They put the money in an envelope and put it in the mail addressed to this poor unfortunate old lady.

Next day she got the envelope, opened it, saw the money and counted £95. But she was so upset she sat down to write another letter: "Dear God. Today I received £95 in the post. I wrote to you and asked for £100, and I know it was you who sent me the money. Those thieving swines at the post office must have stolen £5'!!!

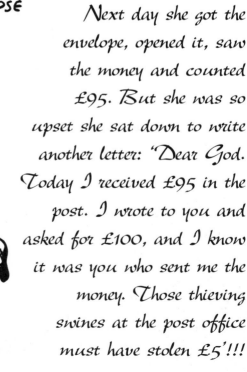

DEAR MADAM, I HAVE JUST DEALT WITH THOSE THIEVING SWINES AT THE POST OFFICE. YOURS. GOD.

A couple were driving through America on their holiday, when they came upon an Indian reservation. Outside one of the teepees sat an Indian, with a sign above his head saying 'This Indian has the longest memory in the world'.
"How!" said the couple.
"How!" said the Indian.
"What did you have for breakfast 25 years ago today?" asked the man. In a deep voice, the Indian replied, "Eggs".
Twenty-five years later, the same couple were passing the same Indian reservation, and outside the same teepee sat the same Indian with the same sign above his head.
"How!" said the couple.
"Boiled," answered the Indian!!!

I was sitting in a taxi, and said to the driver "King Arthur's Close".
"I'll try to lose him at the next traffic lights," answered the driver!!!

HE THINKS ITS ANOTHER
SWORD IN THE STONE!

What's the difference between a dead dog and a
dead traffic warden lying in the road?
There are skid-marks in front of the dog!!!

A drunk walked into the dentist, and said, "Take all my teeth out!"
So the dentist did as he was asked and pulled all the drunk's teeth out.
After the operation, the drunk looked at his mouth in the mirror and
exclaimed, "April Fool! I only wanted a haircut"!!!

What's the difference between unlawful and illegal?
Unlawful is against the law, and illegal is a sick bird!!!

Mother to daughter:
"I don't care if the kitchen wall does have
a crack in it. Will you please stop telling
everyone you come from a broken home?!"

A rep from Pepsi went to see the Pope.
"Listen, Pope," he said, "if you change one word
in the Lord's Prayer, my company will donate millions
of dollars to the Church. If you could say 'Give us
this day our daily Pepsi' we'll pay you more money
than you ever thought possible!"
The Pope pondered, and called in his Chief Advisor.
"Yes, your Holiness?"
replied the Chief Advisor.
The Pope said, "How long
does that contract with the
bread firm have to run?"!!!

A man in a restaurant ordered a cup of coffee.

"Yuk, this coffee's disgusting – it tastes like mud!"

"I'm not surprised," said the waiter,

"it was only ground this morning"!!!

A man had an accident and broke most of the bones in his right hand.
As the doctor was setting his hand in plaster, the man asked,
"Tell me doc, will I be able to play the piano when it's fixed?"
"Yes, of course you will," replied the doctor.
"That's brilliant," said the man, "I couldn't play it before"!!!

Why do women live longer than men?
Because they don't have wives!!!

A man was sitting at his table in a restaurant
when he called the waiter over. He asked him,
"Is it customary to tip waiters here?"
"It certainly is," replied the waiter.
"Well, how about tipping me then," asked
the man. "I've been waiting here for two hours"!!!

What do you call a nun with
a washing machine on her head?
Sister Matic!!!

Scientists and archaeologists have
just discovered a buried Roman fort
in Mid Wales with an electricity
supply. When asked for his reaction
to the discovery, the chief scientist in
charge of the dig said, "Quite frankly,
I was shocked"!!!

A man went to the doctor.
"Doctor, I can feel myself shrinking every day –
what can you do to help me?"
"There's nothing I can do just now," replied the
doctor, "you'll have to be a little patient"!!!

This fella walked into the butcher's
and asked, "Have you got any oxtails?"
The butcher replied, "Once upon a time,
there was a mammy ox, a daddy ox, and a baby ox..."!!!

One day in the old Wild West, a cat strolled between two gunslinging gunfighters, and had his leg shot off. The cat quickly limped off to the hills, where for five years it learnt how to shoot a gun. Then one day the cat returned to the town with a Colt 45. When it walked into the saloon, everyone held their breath.
"What do you want, buddy?" enquired the sheriff.
The cat replied, "I've come for the man who shot ma paw"!!!

A Pembrokeshire potato went home one day, and told her father she was getting married.
"Oh, I hope it's to a King Edward or a Royal Jersey or someone nice like that!" her father said.
"No," she replied, "his name is Harry Carpenter."
"You can't marry him," retorted her dad, "he's only a common 'tato!"

A bank robber went into a bank and handed over
a note saying, 'Give me the money or you're dead'.
The bank clerk said, "Alright Paddy, I'll give you the money."
The robber replied, "How did you know I was Irish?"
"You've sawn off the wrong end of the shotgun!"

"Any jobs?" asked a duck who went to look for work at the Job Centre.
The Manager was amazed, and exclaimed, "A talking duck!"
"Yes," said the duck, "any jobs?"
"Just one minute, while I make a call," said the Manager.
He phoned the circus and said, "It's the Job Centre here –
I've got a talking duck, can you use him?"
"Use him?" said the circus man, "Of course we can, send
him over. Three hundred pounds a week entertaining the kids."

The Manager promptly
returned to the duck.
"I've got you a job," he said,
"with the circus. Three
hundred pounds a week,
entertaining the kids."
"I can't do that," said
the duck.
"Why not?" asked
the Manager.
"I'm a bricklayer,"
replied the duck!!!

Have you ever wondered if
Germans get British Measles?

A man sat on a park bench next to another man
who had a dog sitting on the floor by his feet.
"Does your dog bite?" enquired the first man.
"He's never bitten me," came the reply.
So the first man leaned forward to smooth
the dog – which took half his hand off.
"I thought you said your dog didn't bite!"
"That's not my dog," replied the other man!!!

Which word is always pronounced wrong?
Wrong (of course)!

What's the definition of childish?
I'm not telling you!

A housewife woke her little five-year-old for his first day at school. "Come on Tommy, today we begin school, and if you work hard, you can leave when you're sixteen."
The kid started crying, "I don't want to go to school".
His mam dragged him out of bed kicking and shouting.
She finally got him dressed. By now he was crying frantically. She pulled him out into the street and half carried, half marched him to the school gate. He had cried so much by now that he was exhausted. His mam left him with his new teacher, and turned to walk away. Tommy looked at his mam with a tear in his eye and said, "Don't forget to come back and get me when I'm sixteen"!!!

Two ships collided in the ocean. One was carrying a cargo of green paint, and the other was carrying a load of red paint. Both crews are said to be marooned.

Last January this chap went to a private doctor for a check-up. The doctor told him, "I've some bad news for you – you've only got six months to live."

The chap replied, "Oh God, no! I can't afford to pay your bill until the end of the year".

The doctor answered, "Okay then, I'll give you another six months"!!!

Paddy and Mick from Belfast won the pools, a cool million pounds. Off they went to London to collect the cheque. While they were walking down the street, Paddy said to Mick, "I'm really starving". So Mick popped into a shop and got two pork pies. A little later they were passing a garage, and saw two Rolls Royce cars in the showroom window. Mick said to Paddy "I'd love one of them". Paddy answered "I'll get one for you – you got the pork pies"!!!

I went to a cannibal dinner last night,
and it cost me an arm and a leg!!!

I was just getting out of the bath last night, when my little boy
came bursting into the bathroom and caught me in my birthday
suit. He looked at a certain part of my anatomy, and said,
"What's that, dad?"
"That's my spaceship, son," I replied.
To which my son said, "It's not very big, is it?"
"Just you wait till it gets close to Mars"!!!

What goes hip dip hop dip?
Morse toad

This kid came up to me once and said,
"Hey mister, give me 50p and
I'll tell you how many people are dead
in that cemetery across the road".
I gave him 50p, and he said,
"All of them," and ran off!!!

This fella walked into the butcher's
followed by his dog. His dog jumped
onto the counter, and started eating
four sausages and two pork chops.
"Is that your dog?" shouted the butcher
angrily, wielding a razor-sharp cleaver.
"He used to be," answered the fella,
"but he's looking after himself now!"

Little Tommy started school this week. After his
first day, his father asked him what he had learnt?
"Not enough," said Tommy, "I've got to go back tomorrow"!!!

What do the donkeys have
for dinner on Coney Beach?
Half an hour – the same
as the ones in Blackpool!!!

A guy was sitting on a
park bench holding his nose.
"What's the matter mate?"
asked a passer-by.
"Seenus" said the guy.
"You mean 'sinus'?"
"No, I was in bed with my best
friend's wife, and he's seen us"!!!

COULD'VE BEEN WORSE. HE BITES
EVERYTHING THAT RHYMES
WITH 'SEENUS'...

This man came home from work ecstatic.

"I've won the pools," he told his wife excitedly,

"pack your clothes, quickly!"

"My winter or summer clothes?" she asked him expectantly.

"Pack them all," he answered, "and bugger off"!!!

A man was sitting in his lounge when a
feeling came over him that he was about to die.
So he moved into the living room!!!

A man walked into a pub and asked the landlord,
"Can I have two inches of lager in a pint glass,
and can you fill the rest up with water?"
The landlord said, "That's a strange order".
To which the man replied, "If you had what
I've got, you'd have to drink that as well".
The landlord stepped away, thinking the man was
full of 'flu, and said, "What have you got then?"
"Two pence," said the man!!!

A fella was walking through the railway station, desperate to know the time. He stopped a man who was carrying two heavy cases. "Have you got the time, mate?" he asked. The man put down the heavy suitcases, and looked at his watch. "Well, it's 12.30 here, 7.30 in New York, the weather's fine, and if you look through the screen at the side of the watch you can see them playing cricket Down Under."

"That's brilliant," said the fella, "would you like to sell it?" "Okay," said the man, "but I want £100 for it." The £100 was there in a flash, and the watch changed hands. The fella was delighted with his new watch, and couldn't stop looking at it as he walked away. Then he heard the man shout and point to the suitcases, "Don't forget the batteries!"

PORTER £250 PER WEEK

This chap swallowed two gallons of varnish.
He died a terrible death, but had a lovely finish!!!

Two farmers met at the mart. The first one said,
"Hey Dai, the horse you sold me last week died yesterday".
The other farmer replied, "Well I told you he had some bad
habits, but I've never known him to do that before"!!!

"How long can you keep a chicken in a deep freeze?"
"Three months"
"Well, I put one in there last night,
and it was dead this morning"!!!

What's pink and wobbly and belongs to grandad?
Grandma!!!

IS THIS THE BACK TROUBLE CLINIC OR HAS HE JUST BOUGHT A SNOOKER TABLE?

A man went to the doctor with a bad back. The doctor told him to kneel down on all fours by the window. "Right," said the doctor, "do the same thing by the mantelpiece, and finally on all fours in the middle of the room." The man asked, "Doctor, will this make my back better?" The doctor replied, "I don't know, but I've just bought a new coffee table, and I can't decide where to put it"!!!

One woman said to another,
"Your dog just bit my little boy
when he was on his bike".
To which the woman replied,
"Our dog hasn't got a bike"!!!

I'd just finished decorating the house,
and my neighbour decided to do his. So he
came round and asked me how many rolls
of wallpaper I'd bought to do the living room.
"Twelve," I said.
My neighbour came back round a few days
later and said, "I've got two rolls left over."
"So have I" I replied!!!

A cannibal was taking a walk
through the jungle with his son,
when an aeroplane flew overhead.
The little boy pointed to the plane,
and asked his father what it was.
"Well son," said dad cannibal, "it's
a bit like a lobster – you only eat
what's inside"!!!

This guy walked into the *Army & Navy Stores* and asked,
"Have you got any of those camouflage jackets?"
"Yes," answered the assistant, "but we can't find them"!!!

Maggie Lanigan was sitting in the front row of the choir, when she overbalanced and fell. She went hurtling from the balcony, down to the congregation below. Suddenly her knickers got caught in the rafters and she started swinging up and down. The priest said, "If any man turns round to look at that unfortunate woman, may the Lord strike him blind". Daddy turned to Riley and said, "I think I'll chance one eye!"

Did you hear
about the Irishman
who wanted to learn
how to water-ski?
He gave up
before he started.
He couldn't find
a sloping lake!!!

Two cannibals were talking. One said to the other, "We had burglars last night". "That's awful," replied his friend. The first cannibal looked at him, and said, "Awful? It was terrible! They don't taste half as good as missionaries!"

Did you hear about the karate champion who joined the army? The first time he saluted he nearly killed himself!!!

Police investigating the theft of a ton of cement, three tons of sand, and a ton of gravel from a building supplier's were asked how their enquiries were getting on. They replied, "We have our suspicions, but no concrete evidence yet"!!!

An Englishman was visiting a Texas ranch for the first time. He asked the cowhand the name of the place. The cowhand replied, "It's the Lone Star Diamond Dust One Man On His Horse Topside Of Beef Walk Tall Ranch".
"Goodness gracious," said the Englishman, "do you have any cattle?"
"No," answered the cowhand, "hardly any survive the branding"!!!

A man went to the doctor because his legs were swollen. He told the doctor that he wouldn't be able to get his trousers on if they grew much more. The doctor said to him, "Here, take this".
"What is it, doctor?"
"It's a prescription for a kilt"!!!

Two fellas at a football match.
"It's jam-packed," one of them said, "I've got to go
to spend a penny, but I'll never get out of here!"
His mate suggested, "Why don't you do it in
that man's pocket next to you?"
"Don't be stupid," said the man, "he'll feel it!"
His mate replied "Well, you didn't!"

What lies at the bottom
of the sea and trembles?
A nervous wreck!!!

A fella walked into the doctor's. The doctor said,
"I've got good news and bad news for you".
"Give me the good news," replied the man.
"You've got 24 hours to live," said the doctor.
"What's the bad news?" asked the man.
"I should have told you yesterday"!!!

A lad in a disco asked a youg girl in a mini skirt to dance. She was gorgeous and he was totally thrown aback when she accepted. They danced close to each other, and the boy said, "You're a typist, aren't you?"

"Yes," answered the girl, "how did you know?"

"I can tell by the way your fingers are running up my back".

Then she asked him, "Do you work in a garage?"

"Yes, I'm a mechanic," he replied, "how did you know?"

She said "Your jack has just lifted my mini"!!!

This guy went to the doctor's.
He said, "I've got a left toe on my right foot, and a right toe on my left foot".
"You've got mixermatoeses," said the doctor!!!

A Polish fella walked into the optician's.
The optician said, "Read that middle line".
The Pole answered, "Read it? I know him!"

Four drunks in a car were stopped
by the police, a Welshman, a Scot,
an Englishman, and an Irishman.
The policeman turned to the Englishman
and asked his name.
"George," answered the Englishman.
"Which day were you born?" enquired
the policeman.
"On St George's Day, sir," replied
the Englishman. The policeman then
asked the Scot his name.
"Andrew, sir," he replied, "born on
St Andrew's Day."
The Welshman immediately said
his name was David, born on St
David's Day. Finally, the policeman
turned to the Irishman, and said,
"I suppose your name is Patrick?"
"No," came the reply,
"it's Pancake"!!!

THE MARTYRDOM OF
ST. PANCAKE

BOOKS FROM BBC CYMRU WALES MARKETING

COLIN PRESSDEE'S STREETWISE COOKERY

Out of the Streetlife radio studio, Colin Pressdee, BBC Wales' radio chef, appears in print with a selection of his most versatile and interesting popular recipes.

96 pages with 19 colour photographs
£4.75

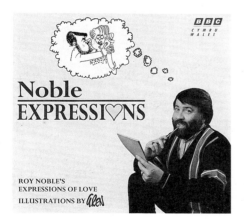

NOBLE EXPRESSIONS

Inspired by his listeners' birthday and anniversary dedications, Radio Wales' Roy Noble has composed countless romantic poems to embellish such happy occasions. Illustrated by Gren, Noble Expressions brings together some of the best of those love muses heard over the airwaves.

60 pages, fully illustrated
£3.50

AVAILABLE FROM ALL GOOD BOOKSELLERS OR DIRECTLY FROM
BBC CYMRU WALES MARKETING, PO BOX 7000, CARDIFF CF5 2YQ